Discovering and Living Out God's
Design for Our Role

Biblical Portrait of Grandparenthood

Deborah Haddix

Biblical Portrait of Grandparenthood: Discovering and Living Out God's Design for Our Role

Requests for information should be sent to:
Deborah Haddix
P.O. Box 8293
West Chester, OH 45069
www.deborahhaddix.com

ISBN: 9781795354400

Contents

There was a time when the word "grandparent" evoked images of rocking chairs, big meals around the family table, gray hair, and wrinkles.

My, how things have changed! Consider the following. Recent data indicates about one-third of all adults are grandparents, their average age is 64, and the average age for becoming a grandparent is around 47. These facts alone certainly broaden the scope of our image beyond rocking chairs and wrinkles.

Add to this that about half of all grandparents are still working, around 55% of those who are homeowners no longer have a mortgage, and Americans aged 55-64 have the highest net worth of any age group. Now, not only has our image of a grandparent become fuzzy, so has the grandparent's understanding of their role.

Messages aimed at a population with money to spend and time to spare, scream, "Indulge yourself. You've earned it." Our culture proclaims that we are not wanted or needed by our children and grandchildren, and we are encouraged to live independently. All of this, and more, creates much confusion among grandparents regarding their role.

- I've worked hard. It's time for me to relax and enjoy life.
- My children are grown. I've done my job.
- My children can figure this out on their own.
- I don't know how involved to be or what to do.
- I'm not sure what my place is.
- My grandchildren live so far away, I'm not sure how it's even possible to "grandparent" them.
- Does any of this even matter?

Where do we go with all this confusion? The Bible.

> *For by him all things were created, in heaven and on earth, visible and invisible, whether thrones or dominions or rulers or authorities—all things were created through him and for him.*

--Colossians 1:16

God is the Creator and Designer of all. Grandparenting is His idea. He created it, and His Word has much to say about His design for it. Within the pages of the Bible, God defines the role of grandparent and describes how to carry it out. It is here where we find the answers to our confusion and learn what God has to say about grandparenting.

If you long to understand God's design for grandparenting and yearn to grandparent well for the glory of God, I invite you to join me in exploring what His Word has to say about the subject.

I am praying that God will do a mighty work in the lives of grandchildren all over the world through grandparents committed to His biblical design, and I am praying that you will fulfill your God-assigned role with purpose and intent.

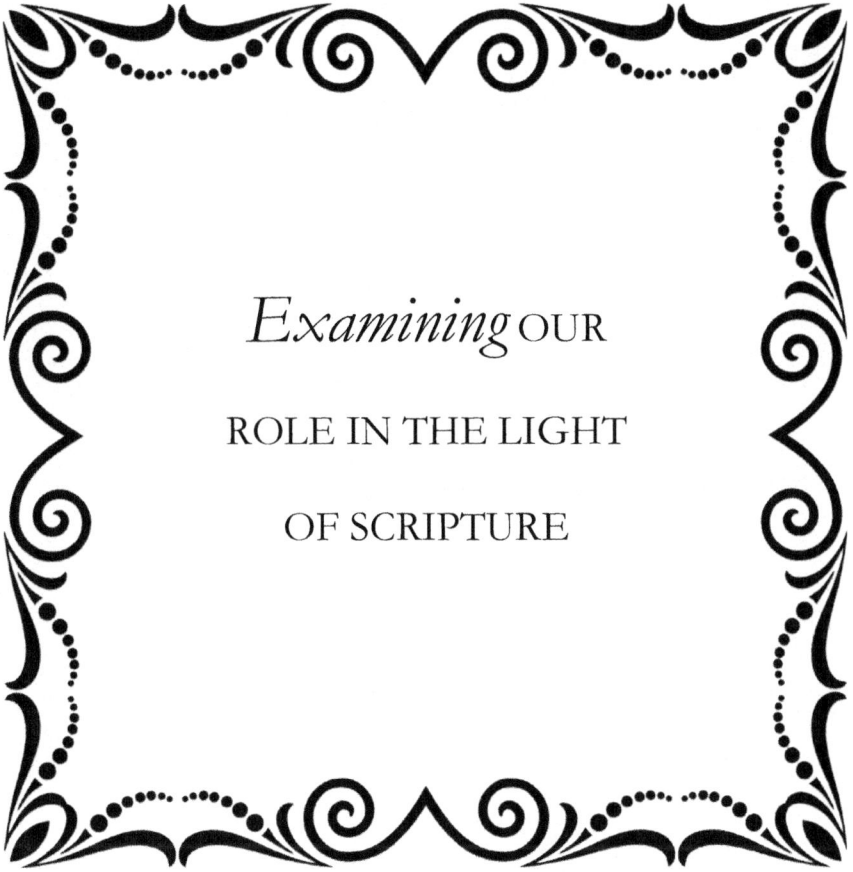

Examining OUR

ROLE IN THE LIGHT

OF SCRIPTURE

"Grandparenting is a grand call—

a divine call,

if I understand it correctly,

that must not be wasted."

Cavin Harper
Courageous Grandparenting[1]

The Scriptures on the pages of this book express God's heart for grandparents. Together they provide a biblical portrait of a godly grandparent.

The questions that follow each verse or passage are designed to help you evaluate how well you are applying God's Word in your role of grandparent. Don't hurry through them. Spend some time here. Use the questions as a tool for self-reflection – meditate, apply, respond to the Lord. Ask Him to open your heart and to help you see areas where He wants to grow you and make you a grandparent after His own design.

To get the most out of this book, you may want to focus on one verse or passage each day. Ask God to show you how your grandparenting measures up to that particular aspect of His design. As you work through the book, consider highlighting two, three, or four Scriptures that reveal specific areas of need in your role of grandparent. Engage more deeply with those Scriptures, engrafting them into your heart and life.

WHAT IS THE ROLE OF A GRANDPARENT?

A good man leaves an inheritance to his children's children, but the sinner's wealth is laid up for the righteous (Proverbs 13:22).

Am I being intentional about the inheritance I am leaving for my grandchildren?

What inheritance am I leaving to my grandchildren?

Am I providing my children and grandchildren a financial inheritance?

Am I actively building a rich heritage in Christ that will outlive me?

[T]hat you may fear the Lord your God, you and your son and your son's son, by keeping all his statutes and his commandments, which I command you, all the days of your life, and that your days may be long (Deuteronomy 6:2).

How am I doing with keeping all of God's statues and commandments?

Do I have a multi-generational mindset?

Am I passing a heritage of faith in Christ to future generations?

How am I going about the task of passing a heritage of faith to future generations?

And Jesus came and said to them, "All authority in heaven and on earth has been given to me. [19] Go therefore and make disciples of all nations, baptizing them in the name of the Father and of the Son and of the Holy Spirit, [20] teaching them to observe all that I have commanded you. And behold, I am with you always, to the end of the age" (Matthew 28:18-20).

Have I embraced my role as a discipler?

Am I intentionally discipling future generations?

Am I making disciples of Jesus Christ, who love God and love others?

Am I teaching future generations to make disciples?

WHAT DOES IT MEAN TO "DISCIPLE?"

[B]ecause, if you confess with your mouth that Jesus is Lord and believe in your heart that God raised him from the dead, you will be saved (Romans 10:9).

Do I understand that discipleship is a process?

Am I helping my grandchildren recognize their need to place believing faith in the person and work of Jesus?

How am I doing at helping my grandchildren orient their affections and desires to God's?

How am I helping my "believing" grandchildren grow in spiritual maturity as a Christ-follower?

Be imitators of me, as I am of Christ (1 Corinthians 11:1).

How am I doing at imitating Christ?

Can I say to my grandchildren, "Imitate me?"

What am I doing to help my "believing" grandchildren take on the character of Christ?

And Jesus came and said to them, "All authority in heaven and on earth has been given to me. [19] Go therefore and make disciples of all nations, baptizing them in the name of the Father and of the Son and of the Holy Spirit, [20] teaching them to observe all that I have commanded you. And behold, I am with you always, to the end of the age" (Matthew 28:18-20).

Do my grandchildren believe in the person and work of Jesus Christ?

Do I regularly share the Gospel with future generations?

Are my grandchildren growing in spiritual maturity?

Am I teaching future generations to obey God's commands?

Are my grandchildren sharing the Gospel with others?

Am I helping to equip my grandchildren so that they may introduce others to Christ and help them mature in the faith?

Personal Reflections

_____

_____

_____

_____

_____

_____

_____

_____

_____

_____

_____

_____

_____

_____

_____

_____

_____

_____

_____

_____

_____

_____

_____

_____

_____

HOW IS A GODLY GRANDPARENT TO CONDUCT THEMSELVES?

Great is the Lord, and greatly to be praised, and his greatness is unsearchable. [4] One generation shall commend your works to another, and shall declare your mighty acts (Psalm 145:3-4).

Do I spend time in praise of my great God?

How often do I praise God in the presence of my grandchildren?

Do I make it a habit to share the mighty works of God with future generations?

Are my grandchildren well acquainted with the working of God in our family's history?

Is my life centered on God?

Is my grandparenting God-centered?

Let not sin therefore reign in your mortal body, to make you obey its passions (Romans 6:12).

Is confession of sin a priority in my life?

Does my life demonstrate an understanding of the consequences of sin?

Am I aware that my sin has consequences for my future generations?

Be careful to obey all these words that I command you, that it may go well with you and with your children after you forever, when you do what is good and right in the sight of the Lord your God (Deuteronomy 12:28).

Am I living in obedience to the commands of God?

Does my life demonstrate faithfulness to the Lord and His ways?

For where your treasure is, there your heart will be also (Matthew 6:21).

For I am already being poured out as a drink offering, and the time of my departure has come. ⁷ I have fought the good fight, I have finished the race, I have kept the faith. ⁸ Henceforth there is laid up for me the crown of righteousness, which the Lord, the righteous judge, will award to me on that day, and not only to me but also to all who have loved his appearing (2 Timothy 4:6-8).

In all that I say and do as a grandparent, do I think eternally?

Do I grandparent with an eternal perspective?

How am I making these later years productive ones for the glory of God?

Do I look forward to standing before God?

[W]ith all humility and gentleness, with patience, bearing with one another in love, ³ eager to maintain the unity of the Spirit in the bond of peace (Ephesians 4:2-3).

Does my life demonstrate a spirit of humility?

Am I patient in my interactions with my adult children and grandchildren?

How do I show that I am eager to maintain peace and unity within my family?

Do I willingly offer forgiveness?

Let no corrupting talk come out of your mouths, but only such as is good for building up, as fits the occasion, that it may give grace to those who hear (Ephesians 4:29).

Do I give thought to the words that come out of my mouth?

Am I intentional about speaking words that build up?

How do I speak to my adult children?

Only let your manner of life be worthy of the gospel of Christ, so that whether I come and see you or am absent, I may hear of you that you are standing firm in one spirit, with one mind striving side by side for the faith of the gospel, (Philippians 1:27).

Am I walking in a manner worthy of the Gospel?

Is Jesus Christ my passionate pursuit?

When my grandchildren look at me, do they see an authentic life?

Is my life a powerful example for the members of my family?

To the weak I became weak, that I might win the weak. I have become all things to all people, that by all means I might save some. ²³ I do it all for the sake of the gospel, that I may share with them in its blessings (1 Corinthians 9:22-23).

Is my life shaped by the Gospel?

Do I grandparent for the sake of the Gospel?

Am I accommodating on matters of preference – technology, hair style, changes to family traditions, etc.?

And he said to him, "You shall love the Lord your God with all your heart and with all your soul and with all your mind. [38] This is the great and first commandment. [39] And a second is like it: You shall love your neighbor as yourself. [40] On these two commandments depend all the Law and the Prophets" (Matthew 22:37-40).

Do I truly love the Lord my God with all my heart, soul, and mind?

Am I growing in my love for God and my love for others?

Do I grandparent in a way that helps my grandchildren grow in their love for God and for others?

Give ear, O my people, to my teaching; incline your ears to the words of my mouth! ² I will open my mouth in a parable; I will utter dark sayings from of old, ³ things that we have heard and known, that our fathers have told us. ⁴ We will not hide them from their children, but tell to the coming generation the glorious deeds of the Lord, and his might, and the wonders that he has done. ⁵ He established a testimony in Jacob and appointed a law in Israel, which he commanded our fathers to teach to their children, ⁶ that the next generation might know them, the children yet unborn, and arise and tell them to their children, ⁷ so that they should set their hope in God and not forget the works of God, but keep his commandments; ⁸ and that they should not be like their fathers, a stubborn and rebellious generation, a generation whose heart was not steadfast, whose spirit was not faithful to God. (Psalm 78:1-8).

I am reminded of your sincere faith, a faith that dwelt first in your grandmother Lois and your mother Eunice and now, I am sure, dwells in you as well (2 Timothy 1:5).

Have I embraced a multi-generational vision?

Am I proclaiming the gospel to future generations?

Does my life point my grandchildren to Christ?

Do I spend time in prayer for the future generations?

Am I developing a multigenerational vision for the salvation and sanctification of my family?

For the promise is for you and for your children and for all who are far off, everyone whom the Lord our God calls to himself (Acts 2:39).

And Jesus came and said to them, "All authority in heaven and on earth has been given to me. ¹⁹ Go therefore and make disciples of all nations, baptizing them in the name of the Father and of the Son and of the Holy Spirit, ²⁰ teaching them to observe all that I have commanded you. And behold, I am with you always, to the end of the age" (Matthew 28:18-20).

Do my actions show that I prioritize family?

Has my heart and life been transformed by God?

Am I discipling those in my home and in my family?

Did he not make them one, with a portion of the Spirit in their union? And what was the one God seeking? Godly offspring. So guard yourselves in your spirit, and let none of you be faithless to the wife of your youth (Malachi 2:15).

Have I made my marriage a priority?

Do I actively protect my marriage?

Am I demonstrating the priority of marriage to my adult children and my grandchildren?

Do I understand the spiritual impact that divorce has on children and that divorce increases the odds that children will walk away from Christ?

"Only take care, and keep your soul diligently, lest you forget the things that your eyes have seen, and lest they depart from your heart all the days of your life. Make them known to your children and your children's children— (Deuteronomy 4:9).

Am I intentional with the care of my soul?

Do I have a "soul care" plan?

Which of the spiritual disciplines am I engaging in as a means for spending time with God?

Which of the spiritual disciplines could I engage with more?

How am I sharing the importance of soul care with my grandchildren?

Am I teaching them ways to care for their own soul?

HOW DOES A GRANDPARENT DILIGENTLY CARE FOR THEIR SOUL?

Keep your heart with all vigilance, for from it flow the springs of life (Proverbs 4:23).

What do I love most in life?

What values do my daily choices exhibit to future generations?

Is my love for Jesus obvious to my grandchildren?

Finally, brothers, whatever is true, whatever is honorable, whatever is just, whatever is pure, whatever is lovely, whatever is commendable, if there is any excellence, if there is anything worthy of praise, think about these things (Philippians 4:8).

What do I spend my time thinking about?

When my mind wanders, what do I find myself thinking about?

How much of my thought life is shaped by Philippians 4:8?

How much is shaped by culture?

Do I rationalize my inappropriate thoughts?

Have I set personal guidelines for how I spend my time?

Let no corrupting talk come out of your mouths, but only such as is good for building up, as fits the occasion, that it may give grace to those who hear (Ephesians 4:29).

Do I have a habit of criticizing others?

Am I prone to critical and negative speech?

Do my words build others up?

Is my tone one of grace?

What do my grandchildren hear when I open my mouth?

This Book of the Law shall not depart from your mouth, but you shall meditate on it day and night, so that you may be careful to do according to all that is written in it. For then you will make your way prosperous, and then you will have good success (Joshua 1:8).

Do I spend time in the Bible on a consistent basis?

Is my reading of the Bible done out of love for God and a desire to spend time with Him?

Am I memorizing Scripture?

Am I meditating on God's Word? What does that look like?

What other ways do I employ for digging in and knowing God's Word?

Continue steadfastly in prayer, being watchful in it with thanksgiving (Colossians 4:2).

Am I consistent in prayer?

Is prayer an "essential" in my life?

Are my prayers a list of "I wants?"

Do I engage in the spiritual discipline of prayer so that I can know God better?

As a deer pants for flowing streams, so pants my soul for you, O God. ² My soul thirsts for God, for the living God. When shall I come and appear before God (Psalm 42:1-2)?

What do I know about my soul and its needs?

Do I have a plan for refreshing my thirsty soul?

Do I engage in the spiritual disciplines as a means for spending time with God and knowing Him more?

Is my relationship with God my first priority?

Personal Reflections

_____

_____

_____

_____

_____

_____

_____

_____

_____

_____

_____

_____

_____

_____

_____

_____

_____

_____

_____

_____

_____

_____

_____

_____

_____
_____
_____
_____
_____
_____
_____
_____
_____
_____
_____
_____
_____
_____
_____
_____
_____
_____
_____
_____
_____
_____
_____
_____
_____

WHAT IS GOD'S PLAN FOR ME AS A GRANDPARENT?

Him we proclaim, warning everyone and teaching everyone with all wisdom, that we may present everyone mature in Christ. [29] For this I toil, struggling with all his energy that he powerfully works within me (Colossians 1:28-29).

Is the spiritual maturity of my grandchild a priority in my life?

Do I know the Word of God in order that I may impart wisdom to my grandchildren?

Am I actively discipling my grandchildren?

What am I doing to help future generations develop Christlike character?

Are God-stories and teaching part of my regular interaction with my grandchildren?

My son, give me your heart, and let your eyes observe my ways (Proverbs 23:26).

Do I understand that God's design for the grandparent/grandchild relationship is long-term, giving it an advantage over all other relationships except parent/child?

Am I being intentional to build a deep relationship with my grandchildren?

Does my life say, "Watch me. Imitate me?"

And he will turn the hearts of fathers to their children and the hearts of children to their fathers, lest I come and strike the land with a decree of utter destruction" (Malachi 4:6).

Am I developing strong heart connections with members of my family?

How am I communicating regularly with my grandchildren so that healthy relationships centered on Jesus are built and maintained?

In what ways am I working to build deep connections with my children and grandchildren?

But as for you, teach what accords with sound doctrine. ² Older men are to be sober-minded, dignified, self-controlled, sound in faith, in love, and in steadfastness. ³ Older women likewise are to be reverent in behavior, not slanderers or slaves to much wine. They are to teach what is good, ⁴ and so train the young women to love their husbands and children, ⁵ to be self-controlled, pure, working at home, kind, and submissive to their own husbands, that the word of God may not be reviled. ⁶ Likewise, urge the younger men to be self-controlled (Titus 2:1-6).

Am I actively involved in discipling my grandchildren?

Am I carrying out my responsibility to disciple future generations within my church family?

Does my training of the younger generations include the sharing of biblical wisdom, guidance, and instruction?

A good name is better than precious ointment…(Ecclesiastes 7:1a).

What is the biblical definition of a good name?

Am I being intentional about establishing a good name?

How am I presenting the gift of a good name to my family?

For from within, out of the heart of man, come evil thoughts, sexual immorality, theft, murder, adultery, [22] coveting, wickedness, deceit, sensuality, envy, slander, pride, foolishness. [23] All these evil things come from within, and they defile a person" (Mark 7:21-23).

When it comes to my grandchildren, do I sometimes forget that all humanity is inclined toward evil?

Does the truth that children carry within them a heart ready for sin affect my grandparenting?

Is it my tendency to try to control my grandchildren's environment and shield them from evil?

Do I see my task one of behavior modification or one of addressing the core sinfulness of the heart?

Does my grandparenting aim for the heart?

[A]nd behold, a voice from heaven said, "This is my beloved Son, with whom I am well pleased" (Matthew 3:17).

Does my speech build up?

Do my children and grandchildren hear words of affirmation in my speech?

Is "love" clearly communicated to my family?

How often do I say the words "I love you" to my family members?

So God created man in his own image, in the image of God he created him; male and female he created them (Genesis 1:27).

How do I treat the members of my family?

Do I treat each member like they are an image-bearer of God?

Do I show preferences among my children or grandchildren?

Am I guilty of treating any of my grandchildren in a way that does not convey to them that they are one of God's image-bearers (special needs, unwanted pregnancy, defiant, tattoo-covered, etc)?

But if anyone does not provide for his relatives, and especially for members of his household, he has denied the faith and is worse than an unbeliever (1 Timothy 5:8).

Am I the first to help when a member of my family has a need?

Am I willing to invest even when it hurts?

Have I bought into culture's message that now is the time to indulge myself?

For even when we were with you, we would give you this command: If anyone is not willing to work, let him not eat (2 Thessalonians 3:10).

Am I prone to stepping in and bailing out family members at the first impulse?

Do I step back and consider each situation before offering assistance?

Have I been guilty of enabling a family member's poor choices?

Do I love generously but with discernment?

Love is patient and kind; love does not envy or boast; it is not arrogant [5] or rude. It does not insist on its own way; it is not irritable or resentful; [6] it does not rejoice at wrongdoing, but rejoices with the truth. [7] Love bears all things, believes all things, hopes all things, endures all things (1 Corinthians 13:4-7).

Am I inflexible?

Do I insist that things be done my way?

Do my daily actions demonstrate love to my grandchildren?

Am I my children and grandchildren's biggest cheerleader?

Does my love for my family members fluctuate according to their actions?

Do I love unconditionally even when my children and grandchildren make unwise choices?

Let all bitterness and wrath and anger and clamor and slander be put away from you, along with all malice. [32] Be kind to one another, tenderhearted, forgiving one another, as God in Christ forgave you (Ephesians 4:31-32).

Is it my habit to try to "fix" my children and grandchildren?

Do I hold grudges?

In the same way that God offered forgiveness to me, do I offer it to others?

When I have been offended, do I consider forgiveness a choice?

Do my children and grandchildren hear me say the words, "Please forgive me. I forgive you?"

I am reminded of your sincere faith, a faith that dwelt first in your grandmother Lois and your mother Eunice and now, I am sure, dwells in you as well (2 Timothy 1:5).

Does sincere faith dwell in me?

How do I offer stability and strength to future generations?

Do I actively remind my grandchildren that God is sovereign and uses everything for good and for His glory?

Which of my life experiences can I use to validate the truths of the Bible for my grandchildren?

Do I make it a point to share my testimony and God-stories with my children and grandchildren?

Convinced of this, I know that I will remain and continue with you all, for your progress and joy in the faith, ²⁶ so that in me you may have ample cause to glory in Christ Jesus, because of my coming to you again (Philippians 1:25-26).

Do I spend intentional time with my children and grandchildren?

Am I using my God-given breath to help my grandchildren glory in Christ?

How am I teaching future generations to fight for joy in Jesus?

So teach us to number our days that we may get a heart of wisdom (Psalm 90:12).

Does my life model godliness for my children and grandchildren?

Am I being intentional to model a life of godliness?

When my grandchildren look at me, do they see a life lived for Christ?

Am I a model of wise decision-making?

Do I respond to suffering in a way that models godliness for future generations?

How am I teaching my grandchildren to number their days?

Does my life say, "Imitate me?"

Therefore you shall keep his statutes and his commandments, which I command you today, that it may go well with you and with your children after you, and that you may prolong your days in the land that the Lord your God is giving you for all time"
(Deuteronomy 4:40).

Am I living in obedience to God?

What do my grandchildren see when they look at my life?

How am I exhorting my children and grandchildren to live a life of obedience to God?

What influence am I having on future generations?

Am I making sure to warn my grandchildren of the consequences of sin?

Is my life worthy of imitation?

Therefore, as you received Christ Jesus the Lord, so walk in him, ⁷ rooted and built up in him and established in the faith, just as you were taught, abounding in thanksgiving. ⁸ See to it that no one takes you captive by philosophy and empty deceit, according to human tradition, according to the elemental spirits of the world, and not according to Christ (Colossians 2:6-8).

What am I doing to root, build up, and establish my faith?

Am I actively and deliberately teaching the essential truths of the Christian faith to my grandchildren?

Am I involved in training future generations to defend their faith against deceptive and competing belief systems?

How am I helping my grandchildren develop a biblical worldview?

The fear of the Lord is the beginning of knowledge; fools despise wisdom and instruction (Proverbs 1:7).

Does my life exhibit a reverential awe of the Lord?

Do I seek wisdom and instruction?

Am I a source of wisdom for future generations?

[A]nd I have seen among the simple, I have perceived among the youths, a young man lacking sense, (Proverbs 7:7).

Am I helping to guide the young people in my life?

Does my life communicate wisdom?

Am I a source of wisdom who is helping to teach future generations?

WHAT IS WISDOM?

"Everyone then who hears these words of mine and does them will be like a wise man who built his house on the rock (Matthew 7:24).

Do I understand that wisdom is obedience in action?

Am I in the Word of God on a regular basis?

Do I live in obedience to Scripture?

WHY IS WISDOM IMPORTANT FOR MY GRANDCHILD?

Blessed is the one who finds wisdom, and the one who gets understanding, (Proverbs 3:13).

For whoever finds me finds life and obtains favor from the Lord, (Proverbs 8:35).

Do I realize that my grandchild's true and lasting happiness is found in wisdom?

Do I understand that wisdom is my grandchild's path to eternal life?

Do I understand that favor with God is found on the path of wisdom?

Personal Reflections

_____
_____
_____
_____
_____
_____
_____
_____
_____
_____
_____
_____
_____
_____
_____
_____
_____
_____
_____
_____
_____
_____
_____
_____
_____

HOW DOES GOD WANT TO USE ME IN THE LIVES OF MY GRANDCHILDREN?

And when your children say to you, 'What do you mean by this service?' [27] *you shall say, 'It is the sacrifice of the Lord's Passover, for he passed over the houses of the people of Israel in Egypt, when he struck the Egyptians but spared our houses.'" And the people bowed their heads and worshiped (Exodus 12:26-27).*

Am I employing the spiritual practice of asking questions?

Am I orchestrating family situations that will lead my grandchildren to ask questions?

Have I instituted, within our family culture, traditions that will encourage members to ask questions?

Do I ask the type of questions that encourage deep thought about the purpose of life?

Am I asking life application questions to help young people make wise choices?

Do I ask a variety of questions (hard probing, unexpected, open-ended, those that require self-reflection)?

Do the questions I ask spark conversation?

I call heaven and earth to witness against you today, that I have set before you life and death, blessing and curse. Therefore choose life, that you and your offspring may live, (Deuteronomy 30:19).

Am I giving my children and grandchildren the gift of blessing?

How do I communicate my approval to my grandchildren?

What things am I doing to show my love and my care to my family members?

Am I treating my grandchildren in such a way that it clearly communicates to them that they have incredible value?

Are my attitudes, words, and actions adding to the life of my children and grandchildren?

You shall teach them diligently to your children, and shall talk of them when you sit in your house, and when you walk by the way, and when you lie down, and when you rise (Deuteronomy 6:7).

Am I being obedient to "sit in your house" by planning family meals?

Am I intentional with family meal time?

Do I use times around the table as opportunities for teaching God's commands and telling His stories?

"Arise, cry out in the night, at the beginning of the night watches! Pour out your heart like water before the presence of the Lord! Lift your hands to him for the lives of your children, who faint for hunger at the head of every street" (Lamentations 2:19).

Do I engage in regular times of prayer for my grandchildren?

Am I taking my concerns about my grandchildren to the Lord in prayer?

Am I praying specifically for the needs of my children and grandchildren?

Do I pray fervently with the understanding that it is God alone who changes hearts?

"Only take care, and keep your soul diligently, lest you forget the things that your eyes have seen, and lest they depart from your heart all the days of your life. Make them known to your children and your children's children— (Deuteronomy 4:9).

[T]hat you may fear the Lord your God, you and your son and your son's son, by keeping all his statutes and his commandments, which I command you, all the days of your life, and that your days may be long (Deuteronomy 6:2).

Do I read the Bible with my grandchildren?

Am I engaging in discussions about the Bible with my children and grandchildren?

Am I teaching the truths of Scripture to future generations?

Am I making use of technology to come up with ways to read and discuss the Bible with my long-distance grandchildren?

He established a testimony in Jacob and appointed a law in Israel, which he commanded our fathers to teach to their children, ⁶ that the next generation might know them, the children yet unborn, and arise and tell them to their children, (Psalm 78:5-6).

Am I actively teaching multiple generations to obey God's commands?

Do I take care to explain Bible passages clearly and biblically?

Am I engaging my grandchildren in the teaching process?

Am I purposeful in helping future generations apply God's truth to their life?

We will not hide them from their children, but tell to the coming generation the glorious deeds of the Lord, and his might, and the wonders that he has done. ⁵ He established a testimony in Jacob and appointed a law in Israel, which he commanded our fathers to teach to their children, ⁶ that the next generation might know them, the children yet unborn, and arise and tell them to their children, (Psalm 78:4-6).

Do I engage in intentional talk about God?

When I am with my grandchildren, do I give testimony to the goodness and greatness of God?

Am I obedient in recounting what God has done in my life?

Do my grandchildren know my God-story?

Am I telling His story and recounting His deeds to future generations?

One generation shall commend your works to another, and shall declare your mighty acts. ⁵ On the glorious splendor of your majesty, and on your wondrous works, I will meditate. ⁶ They shall speak of the might of your awesome deeds, and I will declare your greatness. ⁷ They shall pour forth the fame of your abundant goodness and shall sing aloud of your righteousness. ⁸ The Lord is gracious and merciful, slow to anger and abounding in steadfast love. ⁹ The Lord is good to all, and his mercy is over all that he has made. ¹⁰ All your works shall give thanks to you, O Lord, and all your saints shall bless you! ¹¹ They shall speak of the glory of your kingdom and tell of your power, ¹² to make known to the children of man your mighty deeds, and the glorious splendor of your kingdom (Psalm 145:4-12).

Am I commending God's works to future generations?

Do I declare His greatness and pour forth the fame of His abundant goodness?

Do I tell my grandchildren about the glory of God's kingdom?

Do I declare His power and His wonders?

Do I proclaim the attributes of God?

Am I helping my grandchildren get to know God?

For although they knew God, they did not honor him as God or give thanks to him, but they became futile in their thinking, and their foolish hearts were darkened. [22] Claiming to be wise, they became fools, [23] and exchanged the glory of the immortal God for images resembling mortal man and birds and animals and creeping things (Romans 1:21-23).

Am I sharing the Gospel with future generations?

Am I proclaiming God as the Creator, holy and perfect?

Am I deliberate in sharing with my grandchildren the truth of the Bible – that man has rebelled against God, and God will not ignore or excuse sin?

Am I a vessel that carries the Gospel to future generations?

Do I model the giving of honor and thanks to God for my grandchildren?

A good man leaves an inheritance to his children's children, but the sinner's wealth is laid up for the righteous (Proverbs 13:22).

What inheritance am I leaving to my grandchildren?

Am I passing on a good family name?

Am I investing financially in the lives of my grandchildren?

Am I leaving them with the Gospel of Jesus Christ?

Will I leave them a written personal or family history?

What plan do I have in place for leaving a heritage of faith to my children and grandchildren?

We will not hide them from their children, but tell to the coming generation the glorious deeds of the Lord, and his might, and the wonders that he has done. [5] He established a testimony in Jacob and appointed a law in Israel, which he commanded our fathers to teach to their children, [6] that the next generation might know them, the children yet unborn, and arise and tell them to their children, [7] so that they should set their hope in God and not forget the works of God, but keep his commandments; (Psalm 78:4-7).

What legacy am I building for my family?

Do I want to be known as a Christ-follower?

Will my legacy be one of taking the Great Commission of Christ seriously?

Would I like our family to be known as a family that loved each other deeply, prayed for, cared for, encouraged, and supported one another?

Do I want to be known as a disciple-maker?

Will my legacy be that I prayed regularly for my grandchildren?

Would I like to be known as a giver of time rather than a giver of gifts?

What plan do I have in place for building a legacy for my family?

Personal Reflections

GRANDPARENTING

WITH

Wisdom

*"Grandparents have the opportunity
to shape the beliefs of future generations,
strengthen the family,
build the church, and
transform the nation."*

Dr. Josh Mulvihill
Grand Parenting[2]

My son, give me your heart, and let your eyes observe my ways. —
Proverbs 23:26

Few grandparents are aware of the influence they have on their grandchildren's lives.

Consider for a moment with me:

there are very few relationships in this world that begin in a child's earliest years and continue all the way through adulthood.

By God's design, the unique and long-term nature of our relationship with our grandchild puts us in a position of influence that is second only to that of their parents. Through our attitudes, our words, and our actions, we have the power to help our grandchildren grow to know, love, and serve Jesus with all of their mind, heart, soul, and strength.

The question before us is: *Are we living — with intention — a Christlike life that is worthy of imitation?*

On the following pages are a series of contrasting statements that suggest specific ways we can live a Christlike life worthy of our grandchildren's imitation. I encourage you to spend some time with these statements, checking the ones that best describe your current attitudes, words, and actions toward your children and grandchildren. Before you begin, invite the Holy Spirit into your time of self-reflection. Ask Him to help you be honest with yourself and to reveal areas where you may need to confess and repent.

Whatever you may find as you work through God's design for grandparenting, do not despair. There is good news! You **can** have more substantial spiritual impact on the lives of your grandchildren beginning today.

Ask God to make you a wise and purposeful grandparent so that you may pass a heritage of faith in Christ to future generations.

DO MY *attitudes* REFLECT CHRIST …

☐ I embrace this season of life as a time for living intentionally for Christ, serving Him, and bearing fruit. (Psalm 92:14-15)

☐ I view the grandparenting years as ones to be celebrated and a sign of God's favor. (Proverbs 20:29)

☐ I treasure my grandchildren. They are my crowning glory. (Proverbs 17:6)

☐ I have received my ministry of grandparenting as a gift from God. (Proverbs 17:6)

☐ My approach to grandparenting is… "I get to!" (Psalm 128:6a)

☐ I am confident that God has equipped me with everything I need to disciple future generations. (2 Peter 1:3)

☐ The Bible provides everything I need in order to do what God has commanded. (2 Timothy 3:15-17)

☐ I am committed to meeting the needs of my family members, no matter if I receive anything in return. (Acts 20:35)

☐ I have purposed to be flexible with my adult children regarding holidays and family traditions. (Philippians 2:3)

… OR SELF?

☐ I have worked hard, earning for myself a life of leisure and self-indulgence.

☐ I spend great amounts of time and money searching for ways to hang on to my youth.

☐ I've done my time. My children are grown.

☐ My grandchildren are the responsibility of their parents.

☐ My approach to grandparenting is… "I have to."

☐ I feel inadequate in my grandparenting.

☐ I am often immobilized by the fear that I don't know what to do.

☐ My willingness to meet the needs of my children and grandchildren is determined by the love and appreciation they show to me.

☐ I am insistent that our long-established holiday observances and family traditions remain intact.

DO MY *words* REFLECT CHRIST …

☐ I build my grandchildren up with words of affirmation, appreciation, love, and sincere praise. (Ephesians 4:29)

☐ I frequently and intentionally offer words of blessing to my children and grandchildren. (Deuteronomy 30:19)

☐ I regularly express gratitude for the blessings I have received from God and from others. (Colossians 3:15)

☐ I aspire to speak wise words that will help to point my grandchildren to Christ. (Proverbs 31:26)

☐ I am quick to hear what my children and grandchildren have to say. As well, I am slow to speak in response. (James 1:19)

☐ I am quick to seek forgiveness when I have wronged one of my children or grandchildren. (Colossians 3:13)

☐ I am faithful to pray for my grandchildren. (Ephesians 6:18)

☐ I take care to speak truthful words to my grandchildren. (Ephesians 4:25)

... OR SELF?

☐ I often tear down my grandchildren with words of criticism, fault-finding, and belittlement.

☐ My children and grandchildren seldom, if ever, hear words of blessing spoken from my mouth.

☐ I am prone to grumble and complain about what I do or don't have.

☐ I am quick to speak what's on my mind and share my own opinion.

☐ I am not a good listener. I am quick to share what's on my mind without regard for what my family members may think.

☐ Rather than admitting fault, I tend to justify myself.

☐ I tend to spend much more time talking about prayer and talking to others about my grandchildren's needs than I actually do in prayer.

☐ I sometimes embellish or exaggerate the truth for my own purposes.

DO MY *actions* REFLECT CHRIST …

☐ I use the Bible as my primary source for learning how to grandparent. (2 Timothy 3:15-17)

☐ My grandparenting is discipleship-oriented. I prioritize the spiritual maturity of my grandchildren. (Matthew 28:18-20)

☐ I am proactive. I grandparent with intention. (Ephesians 5:10)

☐ I employ various means for connecting with my grandchildren in order to build deep, long-term relationships with them. (Ephesians 5:10)

☐ I am building a rich heritage of faith in Jesus as a gift for my family. The decisions I make, the way I spend my time, the things I occupy myself with are God-centered. (Proverbs 13:22)

☐ I make the time to care for my soul through Bible reading, prayer, and other spiritual disciplines, knowing that I cannot pour into my grandchildren what I, myself, do not have. (Deuteronomy 4:9)

☐ I coach my adult children as they learn to parent and support them in raising their children for the Lord. (Deuteronomy 6:1-9; Ephesians 6:4)

☐ I have a God-story to tell my grandchildren, therefore, I am developing my testimony. (Psalm 78:5)

☐ I am intentionally and consistently using discipleship practices to help my grandchildren grow spiritually. (Colossians 1:28-29)

... OR SELF?

☐ I tend to seek out a self-help book or the opinions of others when I am not sure how to handle a grandparenting issue.

☐ My grandparenting is fun-centered. I have no particular goal.

☐ I am reactive. I have no plan for grandparenting.

☐ I don't make an effort to connect with my grandchildren by doing things like mailing packages, making phone calls, or spending one-on-one time with them.

☐ I am building a heritage for my family. The decisions I make, the way I spend my time, the things I occupy myself with are me-centered.

☐ My time with God is often crowded out of my schedule by other things.

☐ I do not concern myself with providing input to my adult children. As well, I often usurp their biblical authority by doing things my way when it comes to my grandchildren.

☐ I'm not good at things like writing out a testimony. It takes too much effort and is too hard, besides no one wants to hear my story anyway. It's not that interesting.

☐ I leave the discipleship practices and spiritual growth of my grandchildren up to their parents.

Personal Reflections

_____

_____

_____

_____

_____

_____

_____

_____

_____

_____

_____

_____

_____

_____

_____

_____

_____

_____

_____

_____

_____

_____

_____

_____

_____

_____

_____

_____
_____
_____
_____
_____
_____
_____
_____
_____
_____
_____
_____
_____
_____
_____
_____
_____
_____
_____
_____
_____
_____
_____
_____
_____
_____
_____
_____
_____
_____

End Notes

1. Cavin Harper, *Courageous Grandparenting* (Colorado Springs: Christian Grandparenting Network, 2013), 23.

2. Dr. Josh Mulvihill, *Grand Parenting* (Minneapolis: Bethany House, 2018), 16.

Other Resources by Deborah Haddix

Pray Powerful Prayers for Your Grandchildren: A Handbook -- This handbook is a valuable resource for any grandparent who desires to be a more effective prayer champion for their grandchildren. *Praying Powerful Prayers for Your Grandchildren* shares a unique and engaging prayer technique that helps the pray-er be more specific and consistent in their prayers. The method is clearly explained in this handbook that is also packed with step-by-step instruction, tips, and other resources for implementation of the technique.

Connect: Passing the Faith (Biblical Grandparenting) (Volume 1) -- a resource for Christian grandparents who are seeking practical ideas for building strong relationships with their grandchildren. The book is filled with pages of ideas, tips, and more.

Praying with Purpose: Taking Your Prayer Life from Vague to Victorious—Prayer is the most precious gift we can give our family, friends and loved ones, and this book offers a roadmap for enjoying and sharing a focused and creative prayer life. For those who often pray vague prayers, this book has many suggestions and resources compiled to encourage and inspire victorious praying.

Soul Nourishment: Satisfying Our Deep Longing for God—a gentle reminder of the importance of soul care. It is also a handbook for today's busy woman—filled with a multitude of easy, ready-to-use resources intended to aid in nourishing the soul.

Journaling for the Soul: Handbook —a valuable resource for anyone in need of soul care. The easy-to-navigate handbook contains a wide variety of both traditional and nontraditional journaling method that span the spectrum of spiritual disciplines.

Digging Deeper KIDS (3 Options)

› Digging Deeper KIDS Methods includes 9 different techniques for helping children engage with the Word of God.

› Kids' Journaling Templates are perfect for the child who is intimidated by a blank page or as "training wheels" for the Digging Deeper Kids Methods.

› The Digging Deeper Kids BUNDLE includes both The Digging Deeper Methods AND The Digging Deeper Journaling Templates.

For more information on these and other resources by Deborah Haddix, visit deborahhaddix.com.

Printed in Great Britain
by Amazon